Ethnic Minorities of China

Xu Ying & Wang Baoqin

translation by Li Guoqing

CHINA
INTERCONTINENTAL
PRESS

JOURNEY INTO CHINA

Counsellor: Cai Wu
General Director: Li Bing
Chief Editors: Guo Changjian & Li Xiangping
Deputy Chief Editor: Wu Wei

图书在版编目（CIP）数据

民族之旅/徐英，王宝琴编著； 李国庆译.—北京：五洲传播出版社，
2007.8（2008.5重印）
（中国之旅）
ISBN 978-7-5085-1100-9

I．民…
II．①徐… ②王… ③李…
III．中华民族-概况-英文
IV．K28

中国版本图书馆CIP数据核字（2007）第064531号

ETHNIC MINORITIES OF CHINA

Compiler: Xu Ying & Wang Baoqin
Translator: Li Guoqing
Planner: Feng Lingyu
Project Director: Deng Jinhui
Executive Editor: Qin Tiantian
Art Director: Tian Lin
Photo Credit: Imagine China, China Foto Press,
    Hong Kong *China Tourism*, FOTOE, Feng Tao
Publisher: China Intercontinental Press (6 Beixiaomachang, Lianhuachi
    Donglu, Haidian District, Beijing 100038, China)
Printer: Beijing Picture in Picture Printing Co., Ltd.
Tel: 86-10-58891281
Website: www.cicc.org.cn
Edition: Aug. 2007, 1st edition, May. 2008, 2nd print run
Format: 787×1092mm 1/16
Signatures: 8.5
Words: 25,000
Print Run: 7001–14,000
Price: RMB 92.00 (yuan)

Contents

Preface

China has a long history behind it, the civilization being an important contributor to the evolution of mankind. China is also a multi-national country. The cultures of its ethnic minorities are vital components of Chinese civilization. Today, the 56 nationalities, including the Han nationality, live on China's 9.6-million square kilometers of territory. Although 55 ethnic minorities take up just 8.41% of the Chinese population, they are widely dispersed over 50% to 60% of the land, mostly on plateaus, grasslands or in forests.

The areas where the ethnic minorities live have beautiful sceneries: grand mountains, deep forests, huge rivers and lakes with abundant natural resources. Along with the Han people, these minorities have added to the profound Chinese civilization with their own fascinating cultures.

Among these minorities, 53 have their own languages, 21 have written ones, and almost all have their own religious beliefs and festivals. The 21 ethnic minorities included in this book represent different areas and different cultures of the minority groups living in China: the Tibetan, Qiang and Tu peoples on Qinghai-Tibet Plateau, the Daur, Ewenki, Hezhen and Mongolian peoples in north China, the Dai, Dong and Miao peoples in the south, and the Uygur, Kazak and Hui in China's west. Their beautiful costumes with unique accessories, diverse food customs, fascinating traditions, celebrations and history represent significant elements of Chinese civilization. Such diversity is the basis from which China, as a multi-national country, continues to develop. China's sustainable development and prosperity can also be ascribed to this diversity.

When you travel with us to the "homes" of these families of China, you will find their life and customs endlessly fascinating and their cultures, ancient and mysterious. No matter where you're from, you won't fail to be charmed. Let's begin our journey now.

Mongolian:
The People on Horseback

◎ Nomadic Life on Grasslands
◎ The Three Necessary Skills of
Mongolian Men
◎ The Ancient *Urtiin duu*
(long-song)

The Mongolian people used to be one of the nomadic tribes on the grasslands in north China. In the early 13ᵗʰ century, the Mongolian people, led by Genghis Khan, unified all tribes on the Mongolian Plateau, and thus formed a group, the Mongolian nationality. Today, the Mongolian people in China mainly live in the Inner Mongolian Autonomous Region, and autonomous areas in Xinjiang, Qinghai, Gansu,

Flocks of sheep and cows roaming on grasslands are like white clouds floating in the sky.

Heilongjiang, Jilin and Liaoning—5.81 million people in total.

The ancient Mongolian Plateau connects the Changbai Mountains and Heilongjiang River in the east, the Tianshan Mountains and the Tarim Basin in the west, the grand Siberian grasslands in the north and the Yinshan Mountains in the south. Geographically, the Mongolian Plateau has a dry grassland climate. As it is in China's north, which is high, cold, dry and snowy, the plateau is not suitable for farming. Yet the vast grasslands are ideal for developing animal husbandry. For this reason, animal husbandry has long been the foundation of Mongolian people, the best basis of their life. For hundreds of years, the Mongolians have lived a nomadic custom of migration of following the grass and water, leaving footprints in the country's many pastures. They lived in yurts that can be easily installed and dismantled. Now most Mongolians have settled down in brick or earthen houses, and grasslands tourism has become a passion.

Nadam, in Mongolian, means amusement and games. Every July or August, a *Nadam* festival is held on grasslands as an age-old custom, a sporting competition to display wrestling, archery and horse-racing skills. These days, it has more contents and, in addition to a

The Lele cattle cart is regarded as "the ship on grassland," which perfectly fits local environments.

Easy to be carried along, put up and wind-proof, snow white yurts make ideal shelters for herdsmen on Hulun Buir Grasslands.

The yurt is bright and colorful inside.

celebration for a good harvest, the festival incorporates trade activities. Traditional wrestling, archery and horse racing are still considered three necessary skills for Mongolian men to possess.

Wrestling is probably the most popular and most loved sport among Mongolian people. After Genghis Khan was made the leader of all Mongolians, he made wrestling a criterion of selecting army generals. Average people made wrestling an important event in their holidays. The outcome of a match does not depend on the wrestler's weight. In Mongolian style, one loses if three body parts above the knee touch the ground at the same time. Winners win titles, "giant" for one who beats all rivals for two years in a row, while "lion," "elephant" and "eagle" are rankings below. In history, wrestling was not only a competition, it was a method of choosing a son-in-law. To Mongolian people, wrestling is a contest of strength, courage and wisdom.

Wrestlers may travel a long distance to the *Nadam* Festival. The champion will win much respect from people and love from girls. The wrestling competition is

Tall and strong, Mongolian wrestlers wear highly characteristic clothes.

an elimination series with just one round between two wrestlers. Wrestlers wear high-top boots, leather vests with decorative metal spikes, very loose pants and red, yellow or blue silk ribbons around their necks. Upon thunderous applause from spectators, they stalk in "eagle steps" around the arena first, brimming with confidence and singing a war song. The winner receives a prize: a sheep, tea bricks or even a beautiful, outfitted stallion.

The horse races are equally compelling. The Mongolian people have a reputation of being "a nationality on horseback." Horses, a fundamental part of their life, are indispensable in whatever they do, whether it's battling, hunting, herding or doing trade. The Mongolians learn to ride horses at a very young age. A high level of riding skill makes life much easier. Through a thrilling horse race, they demonstrate the finest animals and exhibit marvelous riding skills. The two types of horse races are galloping and trotting. The latter is only for adults with sophisticated qualities—beautiful appearance, steady gait and faster gait than the others. Meanwhile, the galloping race may have several hundred juveniles in attendance. It's simple: the first to finish the run will win the prize and praise.

Bows and arrows, necessary in battling and hunting, have been loved since

Mongolian men are excellent archery for generations.

Journeying on camel.

ancient times, and represented manhood. Archery, like horse racing, is also an important program at the *Nadam* Festival. The archery competition has two forms, still archery and archery on horseback; they differ in range, arrows and bows, their weight and length, and pulling force. Archery on horseback is done at a run. Brave Mongolian men, in tight-sleeved robes, bend their bows to shoot on galloping horses. Sometimes several bows may be shot at the same time. Excellent marksmen win resounding applause from spectators.

The Mongolian people sing a unique tune called *Urtiin duu* (long-song), an age-old form characteristic of nomadic culture and local grassland custom. Each line in the tune has two parts, improvised by singers about life experience or feelings, sung at varied rhythms. Most of the lyrics involve the beauty of grasslands, fine horses, herds of camels, sheep or oxen, azure sky, white clouds, rivers and lakes. Generally, *Urtiin duu* is accompanied by a Mongolian stringed instrument called *ma tou qin* (horse-head violin). *Urtiin duu* has fewer lyrics but a drawn-out tune, which sounds very melodic and expressive. What's most special about it is that the singer can sing the high and low tones at the same time, a technique called *hu mai*. *Urtiin duu* is viewed as a living relic of Mongolian folk music.

For hundreds of years, the Mongolian people have sung *Urtiin duu* about life, Mother Nature and for a much-blessed future. When the soul of Mongolian music, the melodious and highly expressive *Urtiin duu* and *hu mai* singing are heard across the grasslands, the special charm of the grasslands is highlighted to its finest details.

Hezhen: Fisherman's Songs across the Wusuli River

◎ Fishing in All Seasons
◎ Fish-Skin Clothes and Birch-Bark Boats
◎ Merry Dog Sleds

In the lower reaches of the Heilongjiang, Songhua and Wusuli rivers live an ancient fishing and hunting ethnic minority, the Hezhen people. Hezhen means two things, people in the east and people living on riverside. Today, the Hezhen people, about 4,000, live in Heilongjiang Province.

Hezhen people make a living by fishing. When the Wusuli River is ice-bound, they use a special net to catch fish.

Every one of them is a master fisher.

In this area, mountains are tall and forests deep, rivers and lakes abundant; all provide favorable conditions for fishing and hunting. Up to and including the present, the Hezhen people living on riverbanks make a living by fishing. Almost everyone of them, old and young, men and women, are good fishers with skills inherited from their ancestors. Their simple tools are no more than forks, hooks and nets. The forks they fling never miss their targets. Their fishing skill on a frozen river is incredible; by just cutting a hole in the ice, they are ready to harvest not only fish but also much joy. In spring, they hunt for all kinds of fish. In summer, they repair fishing tools to get ready for autumn, a month-long golden harvest season. During this season, they fish dog salmon and sturgeon to their heart's content. In winter, they cut a hole to net fish on the frozen river. Fish permeates every part of their life. In the past, the Hezhen people calculated their ages by the number of times they had eaten dog salmon. Fish is

also important to children, whose traditional game is to imitate fishermen "forking" fish.

Dried fish is kept as food for future use.

The Hezhen people are excellent at cooking fish and baking or frying is traditional. They also have a unique practice when they receive guests: they fork up fish with a knife and present it to a guest's mouth. If the guest does not hesitate to take it, he is considered a genuine friend and will be received warmly. Otherwise, he is simply refused entry into the house. Eating fish raw is also their custom. Raw fish meat is often served for guests or relatives, along with shredded potatoes, Chinese chives, pepper, vinegar and salt after being rinsed in boiling water.

Fish is not only their food, but, along with wild animals on land, their clothing material. The Hezhen men wear robes of roe deer hide, with two lines of fish-

bone buttons on the front. The Hezhen women wear long robes of fish skin or deer hide, in a fashion similar to the Mandarin cheongsam. Men and women wear fish-skin boots that are well-suited for hunting or fishing. Making fish-skin clothes is not easy. First, the fish is skinned, then punched and kneaded repeatedly until it becomes very soft; then it is dyed with wild flowers of different colors. Even the thread for sewing is made from fish skin. Fish-skin clothes keep the wearer warm, and are very durable, waterproof and attractive.

The Hezhen people can never do without water and fish. They seldom leave rivers for other places. For hunting, fishing or meeting people in other villages, they use boats as transportation. Their boats are singular, made by themselves from birch bark, some for travelling and some for shipping goods. Those for traveling are very light and can be easily portaged to another river. The travelling boats cannot carry many goods, as they are only suitable for one or two persons to travel quickly or to hunt on water. Meanwhile, boats for carrying things, very popular during the 17th century, have a large

Process fish skin with a unique wooden saw.

capacity, with a pinewood keel covered by birch bark. It takes 15 persons to row the boat for shipping on a longer voyage.

In Northeast China, where the Hezhen people live, winter is long, icy and snowy. Dog sleds are ideal land transportation. Like boats, their sleds' function falls into two categories: those used for shipping are larger, while those for hunting, smaller. At least two, and more likely seven, eight or even a dozen dogs do the pulling. The main rope for pulling is for the head dog, and the other ropes for the rest of the pack, all looped around their necks. The head dog must be trained for his job. Dog sleds can travel smoothly on snowy land or on a frozen river. To travel in a snowy forest, dogs have to wear special shoes to protect them from injury. A dog can pull 40 kilograms of weight; over a dozen of them easily move half a ton. Dog sleds, as the favorite transportation of the Hezhen people in winter, can travel quickly and are capable of covering 100 kilometers a day. Today, dog sleds have a new role: tourists love to ride in them.

The simple, hard-working Hezhen people love music. Everyone can sing, accompanied by their traditional *kong kang ji*, a mouth organ. Songs about their dog sleds and boats express their love of the homeland, memories of the past and longing for a happy future.

Hezhen woman in traditional fish-skin clothes.

Daur: Thousand-Year History of Playing Hockey

◎ Home of Hockey
◎ Shaman: A Bridge to the Supernatural

Daur residential houses in "home of hockey."

The Daur people living along the Nenjiang River in China's northeast practise agriculture, animal husbandry, fishing and hunting. Today, the Daur people are found in their autonomous counties in Inner Mongolia, Heilongjiang and Xinjiang, an ethnic minority of 130,000 people.

By historical records, the Daur people have a connection with the Qidan (Kitan), who lived in north China in ancient times. Are they descendants of Qidan people? Nobody knows for certain. What makes this ethnic group world-famous is their traditional sport: hockey, a sport that can be found presently in many countries. Hockey is the Daur people's pride.

The Daur people have a long history of playing hockey. During the Tang Dynasty (618–907), the sport was called *bu da qiu*. During the Song (960–1279) and Liao (917–1125) dynasties, the nomadic Qidan people in north China began to play it in a form similar to the present-day game. This sport was later lost among other ethnic groups, but has been kept popular among the Daur people, and this traditional sport was called *bei kuo* by them.

When they are working in fields, during a break, they use tree branches as sticks and horse dung as pucks to play a game. On each significant holiday, a *bei kuo* game is indispensable, attended by master players from all tribes. A game held at night is spectacular: the puck on fire, blazing in the wind, flies to and fro against the dark

Packaging soybeans for sale.

sky. In recent years, with this sport becoming popular in China, many good players have left their homelands to play for the country.

The hockey game is closely related to their life. When a girl marries, she will bring a nicely made hockey stick for her bridegroom. The Daur people have many expressions related to this sport, "Don't throw your hat like a hockey ball," "Not much use, only good for a hockey stick," or sarcastically, "Good for nothing when you don't know how to play hockey."

Besides the hockey game, the Daur people are strongly influenced by Shamanism, a word originally from Nüzhen (Nurchen) people, meaning, "a person possessed by a supernatural force." Primitive Shamanism practices include worshipping nature, thunder, lightning, rivers, trees, fire, rocks, reindeer, eagles and birds—all being supernatural to the Daur people. To harmonize their relationship with supernatural forces, the Daur people needed someone to act as a communicator. The task is taken by Shamans, who are able to guide a supernatural being from the heaven, help the sick people recover and exorcise evil spirits. For these reasons, Shamans are held

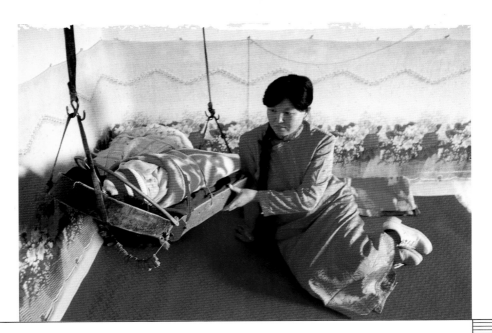

A Daur Woman and her baby on Kang bed. Keeping a baby in a basket hung slant from a beam is their traditional way.

Strength competition.

Shaman Dance.

in high regard by the Daur people.

The Daur people have had little contact with the outside world, and this contributed to Shamanism passing down in its primitive form. On a celebration, a worshipping ceremony, or when someone is sick, a Shaman is invited to present as the key figure on these occasions. When a Shaman conducts a service, he will wear a spectacular robe and use ritual objects to protect himself while exercising his power. His robe has symbolic patterns of living creatures, and over 100 bronze mirrors. With these objects, his robe may weigh up to 75 kilograms. In a ritual, he dances around holding a drum and a drumstick in an ominous manner. This is meant to show respect to supernatural beings and to scare away evil spirits. To the Daur people, the drum he holds is so powerful that all evil spirits will flee at its sound. Seeing such a ritual makes a very rare experience.

Ewenki: The Last Hunting Tribe

◎ Following Reindeer Anywhere
◎ Birch-Bark Fascination

Primeval forests cover the Greater Hinggan Range in China's northeast. In the depths of the forests live the Ewenki people, who make a living by hunting and rearing reindeer. They are the last of the hunting people in China today. Due to ecological changes, hunting has given way to raising reindeer as a major part of their life. Their reindeer culture has lasted for several

Reindeers make the major resource for Ewenki people's living.

They have a deep
"reindeer complex."

thousand years. Most of the Ewenki people, 30,000 in total, live in the Ewenki Autonomous Banner in today's Inner Mongolia, some living in Heilongjiang Province with other peoples, such as the Han, the Mongolian and the Daur.

"Ewenki" means "people living in deep mountains and forests." About 300 years ago, the Ewenki people came from Russia and settled down in Greater Hinggan Range, making a living by hunting. Because the reindeer are a huge part of their life, they are also called "reindeer people."

How long have they kept reindeer? No one knows for sure. But their aged people believe it is as old as their history. Reindeer have big horns with many branches. They walk easily in marshes or snow and feed on moss in forests. Moss is a lower plant growing year-round on the

west side of the mountains, where it is cold and damp. The slow growth of the moss and the fragility of forest ecology make it difficult for the Ewenki people to keep reindeer in a large group.

Reindeers are good transportation in forests or on marsh, for both riding and carrying goods.

The Ewenki people have to migrate frequently. Migration is significant in their life and also a spectacular sight. In summer and autumn, they won't stay in one place for longer than 10 days. In winter, a season to hunt grey mice, they move every two or three days. Usually, men go to a new place first to build an umbrella-shaped shed with 20-some thick pine branches, a shed about 3 meters tall and 4 meters in diameter. In summer, the shed is covered by birch bark while, in winter, by reindeer hide. All the animals will be gathered before a migration. Some with muzzles are tied to nearby trees, reserved as rides if they are gentle or to carry a load if they are not. Before they start, the Ewenki people will remove the cover from the sheds. The crucial aspect is putting out all fire. Fire is very important to the Ewenki people, who usually have one inside and one outside for cooking and

In hat decorated with reindeer horn, the hunter is holding a wolf he has kept.

Hunters in the depth of the Greater Hinggan Range. The fire pit inside is for cooking and keeping warm.

warmth, plus a few bonfires to ward off mosquitoes. So far, not a single mountain fire has ever occurred after they have left a site.

During migration, young women lead the animals walking in front, one family after another; then the aged people follow sitting on top of the reindeer, flanked by adults and children walking on both sides to herd the reindeer. Frolicking dogs' barking, reindeers' panting and people's calling to each other compose an exciting symphony. This is the life of the Ewenki people. The reindeer, forest and Ewenki people have depended on one another in their life for several thousand years.

The reindeer culture can be seen in every component of their life, even on weddings. Parents and relatives will go with the bridegroom to the bride's home. They walk in a neat line, headed by an aged man holding a mystical image in the front, and a person leading a reindeer in the end. The family members of the bride wait in front of their home. When the bridegroom's team arrives, the bride's family presents the bridegroom with a birch box along with a mini-sculpture of a reindeer head as an auspicious token. Then, the young couple selects the two finest animals from the bride's family's herd. The young couple leads them, one for each, to walk three circles before wine is served. After the wedding meal, the bride and the bridegroom take the two reindeer home.

As the forest is becoming smaller, the endangered reindeer are also under protection. One attempt is to rear them in enclosed pens. However, in their evolution, their trotters have long been accustomed to treading freely on marsh or soft earth covered with moss and snow and following them in deep forests is probably what the Ewenki people really want as part of their life.

The Ewenki people are forest people, having a deep love for birch trees. With birch bark, the Ewenki people make instruments and daily utensils, both attractive and practical. Thus, the birch-bark culture was born. Under their nimble hands, birch bark transforms into different items for daily life: basins, boxes, bows, boats and water barrels. With decorative geometric shapes, animal or plant images on them, these objects exhibit reindeer-rearing and hunting culture of elegant, primitive, geological beauty that cannot   be found anywhere else.

Beautiful Burch bark utensil.

Uygur: Little Flowery Hats by the Tianshan Mountains

◎ The Singing and Dancing of Twelve Muqams
◎ Beautiful Costumes
◎ Delicious Food on the Silk Road

The word "Uygur" in Chinese means "unity," a very apt description of the Uygur people's history. Their ancestors were nomadic tribes in China's northwest and central Asia. Today, the Uygur people live in the oasis south of the Tianshan Mountains in the Xinjiang Uygur Autonomous Region, with a population about 8.39 million.

This ethnic minority from the western regions and

"Twelve Muqams" is listed as a "human verbal and non-material heritage" by the UNESCO.

Landscape in Tianshan Mountains, Xinjiang.

central Asia has all the features of a nomadic people. They are happy and excel at singing and dancing. As soon as music from Dombera, a Uygur musical instrument, rises, men and women, old and young, will form a circle to dance. Their famous musical epic called "Twelve Muqams" (meaning 12 big tunes), have a prelude, storytelling, music and dancing parts. It takes a whole day to present it from beginning to end, exhibiting the essence of Uygur music and dancing arts. At the sad tunes from Satar, a special music instrument for this epic, and the heart-breaking singing in a hoarse voice from Muqam artists, and the elegant dancing moves in "imitation" and "competition" parts, no one fails to feel the desolate depths of a desert. The Uygur people describe the "Twelve Muqams" as magic wine or an enchanting picture. Listening to it, aged people become invigorated and sick people on their deathbeds feel at peace, knowing for certain that they will rise to

A young girl is picking grapes at Grape Valley in Turpan.

Meshrep, an amusement form involving singing, dancing and much laughing.

heaven after death. Without the epic, weddings lose their excitement and the desert is simply a lifeless place.

Besides music, the Uygur people have majestic clothing. Men wear a long robe called *qia pan*, a knee-length robe that has long sleeves but no collars or buttons. The ribbon belt they wear is wide and long, capable of holding snacks and personal items. A ribbon belt is usually casual except for holidays or celebrations, during which time it will be replaced with embroidered ribbons in bright colors. The men's shirt is short, closed in front, and often in white, black or dark colors. Young people's shirt has flowery lace. In summer, they wear white and thin *qia pan*, while in winter, they wear cotton-padded ones in dark colors. The Uygur women prefer dresses in bright colors with loose sleeves. The best material is a special silk called Aidelis, described as the most beautiful thing in a desert next only to blooming flowers. This silk has a history of 2,000 years, all made and dyed by hand from cocoons, requiring much time and effort to produce.

All the Uygur people, men and women, old and young, wear exquisitely made flowery hats called *duo*

pa, an important symbol to distinguish them from other nationalities. At a religious ceremony, no one leaves his or her head bare. Having no headwear outdoors is viewed as blasphemous to the heavens. Flowery hats decorated with embroidery, pearls, gold or silver are popular in their life and also make beautiful gifts for friends and relatives.

Uygur foods are well-known. Almost everyone is familiar with their famous meter-long mutton shish kebab. Try it and you won't forget its delicious taste. Its skewer can be 80 centimeters long, with big chunks of mutton meat on a dozen skewers baking in an earthen pit at one time. They are crispy, tender, delicious and fragrant. The whole roast lamb—golden, shiny and crispy outside but very tender inside—is served to honored guests.

Their three meals take wheat flour as the staple

Uygur old man is selling flowery hats.

Early morning in Turpan, *nang* just baked from an earthen pit smells so good.

food. *Nang*, hand-picking rice and baked dumpling are important dishes. They eat a lot of meat, mostly mutton and beef. *Nang* made of wheat or corn flour in different sizes and thickness baked in an earthen pit is their national cake. Golden and crispy, a daily necessity, it can be kept much longer than other food. People say, "Not a single day can pass without *nang*." When the Tang monk Xuanzang travelled west for Buddhist sutras, legend has it, *nang* was the food that helped him cross the Gobi Desert. Now, in many cities of China, *nang* is available at the market as a popular snack.

Hand-picking rice is the Uygur people's pride, called polur, cooked with rice, mutton, sheep fat, vegetable oil, onion and carrots. A sheet is spread out and all the family members sit down beside it for a meal. Traditionally, they wash hands both before and after a meal. They don't use a basin to wash hands, but use water from a pot to rinse

hands three times, then they dry hands only with towels. Used water is collected in a bronze or wooden basin. If they have a guest, the guest is seated at the most honored position. After the meal, a simple religious ceremony is conducted by aged people from the family. It is impolite for guests to rise and leave before the hostess clears away all the dishes.

Apart from these, the Uygur people have many other kinds of delicious foods. If you ever travel to that region, stroll along the Silk Road and enjoy the charms of the Uygur life, and don't forget to taste these delicious foods—you'll love them.

Local food specialties sold in Urumqi international market.

Hand-picking rice is never missing when receiving guests, on special occasions or celebrating a holiday.

Tu: The Rainbow Nationality and Its Unique Songs

◎ The Popular *Regong* Art
◎ Rainbow Costumes
◎ Folk Songs

Most of the Tu people, about 240,000, live in the Huzhu Tu Autonomous County, Minhe and Datong County, east of Qinghai Province, while others live in Tongren, Ledu and Menyuan.

Their northeast Tibet a place forests, pastures rivers climate, homelands are of Qinghai-Plateau, of dense large and many with a mild abundant

Wooden Buddhist sculpture of *Regong* art.

crops and fruit. The beautiful environments have greatly influenced them, giving rise to their brilliant cultural and artistic bent.

In the areas where many Tu people live, artists, either with monasteries or not, are devoted to painting, clay sculpture or wood engraving. They make Buddhist images and frescoes or decorations on lintels, beams or column ends. These artists are called *Regong lasuo*, and their art is called *Regong* art. Many monasteries in Qinghai-Tibet Plateau have their works. Most of their paintings are done in a meticulous-brushstroke style, often in sumptuous colors, characteristic of the Tibetan Buddhist School. On the ends of columns or beams, engraved patterns of a good harvest or strong, domestic animals are often seen. In construction decoration, the artists are probably the most famous. The clay Buddhist sculptures in these areas exhibit obvious attempts by Tu artists to incorporate Tibetan and Han religious features.

The Tu people's clothes are very typical of their culture and can be distinguished in one glance. People call them "a rainbow nationality." White underwear with embroidered high collars and angled fronts inside, and coats of black-trimmed sleeves, black or dark vests, blue loose pants plus embroidered waist ribbons are typical attire for men. Some young men like to have an embroidered pattern on the front of their coats. Some Tu men wear felt hats tilted up both front and back. The clothes for women vary from

Tu people's traditional houses and fields, overgrown with wheat and rape crops, in the Huzhu Tu Autonomous County, eastern Qinghai.

Embroidery art carried on by Tu women for many generations.

place to place, but they are all in bright colors, some in five colors, others in seven. Their ribbon belts are wide and long, with embroidered patterns at both ends. They wear black or purple vests over their blouses, and long skirts or trousers. Young women like red and their skirts are multicolored, while the middle-aged prefer brown, with openings on both front and back. Their slacks are in two colors above or under the knee. The color under the knee represents her marital status. The single woman wears red while the married has blue.

Their embroidery works can be seen on collars and sleeves. Young men like to have an embroidered square pattern on the front of their coats, a pattern of *tai ji* or plum-flower images. Another pattern called "fortune continues to no end" is often seen on belts or collars. Almost everything—a pillow cover, a diamond-shaped cloth worn by babies, tobacco pouch, purse—has embroidery. If a girl is skilled at this, she is looked on favorably by everyone, and is believed a potentially good wife.

The Tu people's unique folk songs fall in two types: "family songs" and "wild songs." The "family songs" include eulogies, mischievous questions and answers, wedding songs and ballads, have fixed tunes, often in two stanzas. Eulogies are melodious and soft, while the mischievous questions and answers are short and succinct, with a pause at the end of each line. The "wild songs" are also called "flowery tunes (*hua'er*)" of a dozen or more kinds. Their "flowery tunes" have similarities with those in Gansu, Qinghai and Ningxia, all being very resonant, high-pitched, fast and unrestrained. The difference is that the Tu people's songs have a bigger variation in melody and a wider range.

Local ceremony to exorcize evil spirits.

Their "flowery tunes" have two, two and a half, or three completed stanzas, two of them having substantial lyrics while the rest having supporting echoes. Each tune is repeated twice, with a drawn-out endnote. If you ever have a chance to visit their area, don't miss the opportunity to hear this unique form.

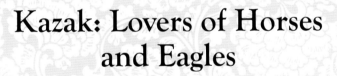

Kazak: Lovers of Horses and Eagles

◎ Training Eagles in Mountains
and on Grasslands
◎ Musicians Who Play Dombera
◎ The Exciting Game of "Girls' Chase"

On a galloping, fine horse followed by hounds with an eagle perched on his arm: this is a typical image of Kazak people on the hunt. They live mostly in their autonomous prefectures and counties in Xinjiang, and also in places of Gansu and Qinghai. Their total population: 1.25 million

Hunter and his eagle.

people.

Their places are surrounded by the Tianshan, Altai and Tarbaghatai Mountains, with Junggar and Ili valleys in the middle, crisscrossed by several rivers and dotted by plateau lakes. The surrounding hills make fine pastures for summer, while riverbanks and hilly lands are ideal for winter pasturing. For generations, the majority of Kazak people have wandered as a nomadic nationality, while a small number have farmed. Because of the environment, most are excellent hunters. They use no firearms but a traditional helper: the eagle. Training an eagle for hunting requires much skill and effort.

The eagle is a ferocious, swift and legendary bird of prey, viewed as a symbol of courage and might for thousands of years. It is not easy to capture and train, yet the Kazak hunters know how.

After capturing a big one with a net, clips or a trap, or taking a baby bird from a nest in the mountains, the

Kazak people's pasture.

At migration, they disassemble tents, package belongings and ship them to a new spot by camel.

Kazak hunters wash its body and stomach repeatedly to get rid of its "wild scent." After being "conditioned" for half a month, the eagle is domesticated. Feeding is a tactful process. Shredded meat is washed clean, held in a leather-gloved hand and revealed a little for the bird to peck. By then, the bird is extremely hungry and at the sight of meat rushes to it desperately. The hunter backs away, step by step, increasing the distance each time, thus forcing the bird to fly to him. Each time, he feeds the bird just half full. When the bird can fly swiftly and perch on his arm to peck the meat, the training is almost completed. To make trainer familiar to the bird, the trainer sometimes mixes the food with his saliva. Up to then, all the training happens indoors. Next comes the more important outdoor training.

When hunting, Kazak hunters keep the eagle a little hungry in order to retain its desire to kill, an age-old lesson handed down from ancestors. The bird is kept blindfolded and its feet chained until a prey is spotted.

Most hunting is done in winter, when wild rabbits, foxes and gazelles are on the move. Each hunting trip is rewarding. Although a hunting eagle is not the largest bird, it is by all means the most ferocious fighter. There

Playing their folk mu[sic] piece Dombera.

Receiving guests at home with tea and special food.

was a popular saying among the Mongolian people when they tried to conquer the central Asia, "A well-trained hunting eagle is priceless, even more than a fine horse." In the past, such an eagle cost more than a girl's dowry.

Hunting on horseback with ferocious eagles and dogs by their sides, Kazak men appear combative. However, otherwise, they are just humorous, happy herdsmen. They have many folk stories to tell, ballads to sing and aphorisms to pass down generation after generation. The best performers among them are called *A Ken*, a name of much respect given to story tellers and ballad singers. They are folk artists but different from those in other nationalities, as Kazak story tellers sing in an improvised manner accompanied by their own musical instruments. Thanks to these versatile artists, the history of Kazak has been preserved.

The Kazak men are handsome, while Kazak girls are pretty. They have a special entertaining game called "girls' chase," where girls find boyfriends of their own free will. The "girls' chase" is held on holidays. Before it starts, participating tribes settle on choosing players

and horses. Their horses are fine, and the rides for girls must be better than those for boys. The pair will go to the designated spot, side by side, and on the way, the boy can say anything to the girl, and can even kiss her. The girl is not supposed to get angry. However, as soon as they reach the designated spot, the boy immediately turns around for a desperate escape. The girl follows in a hot pursuit, brandishing a whip. She means to whip him as punishment for what he has done or said. However, if the girl likes the boy, her whipping is feigned or falls on the young man's back very gently. This form of courtship has enabled many young people to find true love and to marry.

"Girls' chase" on Ili Grasslands.

Hui: Devout Muslims

◎ Entering the Islamic Culture
◎ Unique Islamic Constructions

Compared with other ethnic groups in China, the Hui people have a bigger population. In white or blue hats, the Hui people can be seen almost everywhere in China: working hard and scrupulously

Praying to Allah.

Doing a religious ceremony inside a mosque.

adhering to their religious rules. Actually, the majority of Hui people live in the Ningxia Hui Autonomous Region, some in Gansu, Xinjiang, Qinghai, Hebei, Henan, Yunnan, Shandong, Beijing and Tianjin. Today, the Hui people have a population of 9.81 million people.

Chinese Hui people are pious Muslims and believe in the Islamic religion of the Sunni sect, praying five times a day in the direction of Mecca, saying *shahadah*. Every Friday, they go to their mosque for a religious service and every year they have a month-long Ramadan. A mosque is where they conduct their religious activities. Any Muslim with conditions makes a pilgrimage to the sacred Mecca at least once in his lifetime. Apart from major religious holidays like Id al-Adha and Lesser Bairam, they have other religious occasions during the year.

The Hui people abide by Islamic rules. Every year, they have a month-long Ramadan, during which they can eat as much as they like before sunrise. However, between

Pious Muslims.

The Dongguan Mosque, Xining, Qinghai Province, the largest mosque in Northwest China.

sunrise and sundown, no food or drink is allowed, and personal desires of any kind, prohibited. Of course, babies, the weak, the aged, the sick and the pregnant are exceptions. The last day of Ramadan is Lesser Bairam, which falls on the last day of September by the Islamic calendar. That morning Muslims gather in the mosque for a religious service before they start their celebration. Id al-Adha is another major holiday that falls on the tenth day in December by the Islamic calendar, meaning "butchering livestock for sacrifice." During Id al-Adha, all Islamic families would clean up their houses. All families that possess cattle would butcher some sheep, camels or oxen. In the morning of the festival, Islamic people would tidy their clothes after taking a bath and listen to imam's interpretation of Koran in the mosques. After prayers and rites, all the families will go to graveyard to pay tribute to their late beloved on the day.

Muslims observe many rules in life: no partaking of pork, horse and mule meat or animal blood, no partaking of dead poultry or anything not butchered by an Islamic follower, and no baring of chests or arms before other people.

The Islamic culture is apparent in its architecture, the mosque (*qing zhen si*) being a fine example. "*Qing zhen*" originally meant "simple and unadorned." The Chinese Hui people have added more to its content, being pure, unsullied and everlasting. Their mosque is a place with more than just one purpose, it is a place for the Hui people to clean themselves, perform religious ceremonies and hold religious classes to spread Islamic knowledge and to train Islamic workers. The Chinese Hui people's mosques fall in two categories: one in Arabic style with a

Hui People's
residential house.

dome on top, another in traditional Chinese architectural style, with upturned eaves and lock brackets. No matter what style, mosques are very clean inside, solemn and quiet, with painted plants and relief engravings of Koran and Arabic square-shaped inscribed boards on walls.

Their residential houses look similar to those of local Han people. In the countryside in China's northwest, most of their houses are one level—either cave dwellings

Hui people having traditional food and celebrating their Id al-Kurban.

or brick-and-tile constructions. Most of their houses face south to receive maximum sunshine. In mountainous areas in south Ningxia, the Hui people like to add another floor, commonly called "tall houses." The added space is for a religious purpose and free from disturbance from children. On the lintels of many houses, words from Koran written in Arabic language, mostly being the eulogy to Allah, can be seen. Like their ancestors, the Hui people today still like to burn joss sticks, having moral guides inside their main room, sutra basins on each side, and a Koran ready for a service. Burning joss sticks at home has a dual purpose: one for a pure place and the other to expel evil air.

Kirgiz: Born from a Heroic Epic

◎ Homeric Epic in China—*Manas*
◎ Beautiful Artwork of *Tu xi tu ke*
◎ Countless Uses of Camel Hide

Their places are surrounded by mountains, and for this reason, the Kirgiz people are called "dwellers on mountains." Most of them live in their autonomous prefecture and other counties in Xinjiang Uygur Autonomous Region. Their population: 160,000. Their places are in the depths of the Pamir Plateau and the Tianshan Mountains. Rivers from thawing snow flow from west to east, leaving lush pastures on both sides

Young Kirgiz herder.

Herdsmen singing their
national epic, *Manas*.

ideal for animal husbandry. Some riverbed basins are
suitable for farming, too. Here, on these fertile lands, the
Kirgiz people farm and rear livestock and here, among
these mountains, lands and rivers, the Kirgiz epic, *Manas*
was born.

Manas is a magnificent work, not only just an epic, but
an encyclopedia about their society, history, geography,
life, customs, religious belief, economy, family, arts,
language and literature. It has eight sections, depicting
heroes of eight generations fighting for the unification of
tribes for a common happy life.

The epic is a large-scale work of over 200,000 lines,
each containing an individual story, which is good for
singing and telling. Figures and plots are well-connected,
contributing to a complete and well-knitted magnificent
literature. It has been passed down through history
not in a written form, but by the songs and storytelling
of generations. This priceless folk heritage has been

Kirgiz young women in Xinjiang are doing embroidery.

translated into foreign languages and is known as China's Homeric Epic.

They have not only the magnificent epic of which to be proud, they have other elements, such as handiworks well-known even in foreign countries, drapery, straw objects and camel-hide products.

Tu xi tu ke, the Kirgiz draperies, are age-old objects for

Young people in their holiday best.

house decoration, which can quell the damp and protect walls, and they are attractive and unique. Most of the houses have a drapery on the most conspicuous place on the wall, often 1.2 meters tall and 3 meters long—purple velvet trimmed by black velvet with tassels. Popular images are peaks, waves of water, clouds and plants, which relate to their daily life, their farming and animal husbandry and also the surrounding mountains and pastures. Most of the makers are women.

Camel-hide products are also the pride of the Kirgiz people. Different parts of the hide are made into different handiworks, say, water buckets, pots or bowls. They are d u r a b l e   and attractive.

Children at tug-of-war.

The camel barrel is made from the animal's neck. When a camel is butchered, the neck is scraped of meat and fat to make a hollow roll. Then, the hair is removed and sewn with

thick thread and filled with pressed, solid sand. The barrel-to-be is smoked for a year before the final touch: a round piece of hide as the bottom is sewn together with fine thread—too fine for water to leak—and, finally, with two added handles, the bucket is complete and good for holding 5 to 6 kg of milk or water.

A camel-hide pot is used to carry water and is said to be used by ancestors for washing their hands and faces before they left for a battle. Because it is extremely durable, it is particularly good for horse or camel riders.

Tibetan: On the Roof of the World

◎ Age-Old Tibetan Buddhist Culture
◎ New Looks of Old Tibetan Opera
◎ Fascinating Costumes

The Potala Palace at the center of Lhasa, symbol of Tibetan history, culture and Qinghai-Tibet Plateau.

The Tibetan people, 5.41 million in total, live on the roof of the world, the Qinghai-Tibet Plateau, administratively, in the Tibetan Autonomous Region, as well as in other autonomous prefectures or counties in Qinghai, Sichuan and Yunnan. They make a living by animal husbandry of sheep, goats or yaks. They farm, too, and grow crops such as wheat, canola and

Making a kow-towing pilgrimage on foot from distant home to Lhasa.

Through debates, Lamas are studying Tibetan Buddhist sutras.

Turning the sutra tube, a common religious practice, is for blessings.

peas. Their staple food is roasted highland barley and yak butter.

The Tibetan people are outgoing, warm, courageous and unconstrained. They like to dance and sing about their happy life under the azure sky. The Tibetan folk songs and rhyme are melodious and fast-paced. Their drawn-out tunes are heart-rending. When they sing, they often dance at the same time.

Tibetan Buddhism is the most important part of Tibetan culture. Around the 7th century, Buddhism travelled from India to Tibet. Now, it has over 1,300

Working on *mani* stones.

years of history. Based on Buddhism, Tibetan Buddhism incorporated features from a local, original religion called "*Ben*." Between the 13th and the 16th centuries, Tibetan Buddhism developed rapidly, becoming very popular and active. Many monasteries were built, among them the most famous are the Potala and the Tashi Lhunpo. Tibetan Buddhism has four sects, Gelugpa, Sagya, Kargyupa and Ningma; of these, the Gelugpa, also called the Yellow Sect, is the largest. The Yellow Sect practises a Living Buddha succession system from the two branches of Dalai and Panchen.

The Tibetan people are pious Buddhist followers. They are willing to give their life savings to their living Buddha. On the Qinghai-Tibet Highway, devout followers can be seen frequently kowtowing every three steps on a trip to the sacred Lhasa, which usually takes several years. The Tibetan people carve their sutra on stones, which are called *Mani* stones, often piled up by roads, on

Traditional Tibetan Opera play at Norbulingka.

bridges or on top of a mountain. In very cold weather, they keep the stone inside their robes next to their bodies to draw strength from the stone. The Xinzhai Town in Yushu Tibetan Autonomous Prefecture in Qinghai, built by the living Buddha of the first generation, had over 2.5 billion pieces of *Mani* stones by the 1950s.

The influence from Tibetan Buddhism on the locals is amazing. Their daily life are filled with awe of the Buddha. They have many religious taboos, such as making no noise inside monasteries, no smoking or touching Buddhist images.

The Tibetan Opera is called a living relic, one of the oldest forms existing in China. It doesn't take many props or a serious theater, yet it enjoys huge popularity. A Tibetan play may draw a huge audience from near or far. The Tibetan Opera evolved from local folk songs, poetry, dancing, music and storytelling. With a little preparation, actors begin to act in masks that represent

Mask dancing in a
Tibetan Opera.

different types of characters, evil or good. The characters
have little dialogue but much singing and are joined by a
supporting cast on backstage. A storyteller, accompanied
by clappers in hand, explains the plot to the audience.
The characters sing and dance, accompanied by music.
Because the venue is usually large, their singing must
be very resonant and project to all of the audience, some
of whom are far away. Most of their stories are adapted
from folklore, legends, Buddhist tales and past events.

Tibetan clothing has strong national characteristics—

Lovely Tibetan girl.

big waist, long sleeves and large fronts, varying from place to place in style, decoration, color and the manner in which it is worn. Women's clothing has about 100 varieties. Their hair has many plaits with decorative objects to hang on their backs. Tibetan women wear a lot of jewels—gold, silver, coral or agate on the head, neck, hands and waist. Monks and nuns wear Buddhist outer vestments only.

Very impressively dressed Kangba man.

Dai: Buddhist Temples and Bamboo Houses

◎ Devout Buddhist Followers
◎ Water-Splashing Festival
◎ Elephant-Foot Drums

The Dai people have a long history, with their own written and spoken language, and a population of 1.15 million, most of who live in west Yunnan close to borders with huge mountains and large rivers. Most of their villages are built on fertile, flat lands, overgrown with thick tropical vegetation and precious

Beautiful scene in Dai people's home area.

The temple in Jinghong, Xishuangbanna, Yunnan.

A monk is copying sutra with a bamboo stick on pattra leaves.

Worshiping ceremony of
Dai people.

medicinal herbs. Rice is their major crop. Xishuangbanna
and Dehong are known as "rice granaries in south
Yunnan."

The Dai people believe in *Hinayana*, a sect in
Buddhism, with characteristics of primitive Buddhism.
Hinayana followers seek individual *mukti*. This sect first
came from India, then via Sri Lanka to China's Yunnan.
Every Dai man must spend a period of time as a monk
in a temple. In the past, education was only available in
temples. Only by living in a temple could people receive
education, win the right to establish a family. Otherwise,
he would simply be despised in society. After receiving
a Buddhist title, he could return to a secular life. People
remaining in temples would further study Buddhism, be
promoted and become a lifelong monk.

Their most well-known festival is the Water-Splashing,
which falls on their New Year's Day by their calendar
(in April). By legend, long ago, seven kind-hearted girls
were set on fire after killing a devil king as they could
no longer endure his brutality. People rushed to save

them by splashing water on them. To commemorate the seven girls who rid the community of a local tyrant, on each New Year's Day, people splash water on one another "to get rid of dust and to receive blessings." The Water-Splashing Festival is also a religious one, lasting from 3 to 7 days. The first day is like Spring Festival Eve, the second is for resting or hunting in mountains, and the third day is their New Year. On that day, early in the morning, people change into their best clothes. They bring water to temples to "bathe Buddha." Then, they begin to splash water on one another as wishes for auspiciousness, happiness and good health. Splashing water at the beginning is gentle. Soon it becomes wild without restrictions. Gentle young girls become aggressive and begin a "water fight" with young men.

Their elephant-foot drums are famous. In every Dai village, there is at least one set of drums or more in a variety of sizes. There is a legend about the drums. Long ago, two monks seeking Buddhist sutras came to a Dai Village. They heard beautiful sounds when the birds pecked at fruit in the trees, the fruit fell into the river, and

Water-Splashing Festival in Xishuangbanna, Yunnan.

the fish rose to the surface for food. Recalling what they just heard, the two monks made elephant-foot drums to reproduce the sounds. Usually, a drum has an hour-glass shape, about 1–2 meters in diameter, and is covered by ox or goat hide. The body of the drum is made from a complete log, finished with engravings on its body. Ox-

Working on an elephant-foot drum.

hide ribbons are attached and are tightened or loosened for different notes. Before playing, the drummer will brush some gruel rice on top for better sound effects. They play the drum with fists, palms, fingers and elbows and even feet for varied sounds.

Gracefully dancing by elephant-foot drums.

The elephant-foot drum is an important musical instrument for elephant-foot dancing, and when, joined with other instruments, they display a nice percussion to express happy feelings.

Dong: Grand Song Singers

◎ Singing across the Mountains
◎ The Charm of Unique Drum Houses
◎ Wind-and-Rain Bridges

The Dong people in Guizhou, Hunan and Guangxi grow famous fragrant sticky rice as a major crop. Some, though not many, keep fish farms or do forestry production. Its population: 2.96 million.

Their homeland is commonly called "land of songs

Dong people's unique drum-tower architecture.

Life-like sculptures
on the drum tower.

Inside a drum tower.

Dong girls enjoy singing during a slack season.

and poetry." Their grand songs in multiple parts, unaccompanied by musical instruments, represent the highest in their culture and are invaluable for music and literary studies. The Dong people use songs to record their culture, social practices, etiquette and customs. Their grand songs are unique, with one voice higher than others in succession, so it takes at least three to sing a grand song. Multiple parts, unaccompanied and without a director, are grand songs' main features. Their grand songs may mimic birds, insects or running water from mountains. Most of their songs are about scenes of life: work, love, friendship and the harmony among people or between man and nature. The evolution of their grand songs is legendary. They were born from ordinary people, sung indoors by a group—melodious, slow, gentle, and profound. When their grand songs were sounded, the

music was like a dreamy, ancient voice from the mountain depths, calling on the people, and revealing the history of this region.

For many years, music scholars in the world believed that China had no music of multiple parts or harmony. This belief continued until the 1950s, when a famous musician Zheng Lücheng made a surprising discovery, the grand songs of the Dong people. Their choral performance in France in 1986 was a sensational event and the music world was extremely enthusiastic. Since then, nobody has ever questioned the existence of multiple parts or harmony in Chinese traditional music. Singing a grand song is a huge event, which happens only at major festivals, social occasions or receiving honored guests from afar. Among all, the voice songs are the most outstanding, often named after an insect or an animal like

Cicada or *The Third Month*. The Dong people take their songs as their treasure, culture and knowledge. The one who can sing more songs than others is considered to be the most knowledgeable and the best educated and, thus, highly esteemed. The way they sing is closely related to their life habits, personality, psychology and living environment. Their songs record their history and mirror their culture.

Besides singing, the Dong people are good builders. Their nice stone or wood constructions are very impressive. Among all constructions, the drum houses and the Wind-and-Rain Bridges are the most representative.

The drum house has a special position in a village, which can often be seen at the center of the village or close to its gate. Whenever a big event happens that requires discussion of the villagers, the village head will sit inside the drum house to preside over a meeting.

The Dong grand song has been proudly performed in other countries.

Otherwise, the drum house is a place for entertainment. After a day's work, they may gather around a bonfire inside the drum house to tell stories, play musical instruments and sing ancient songs. On festivals, or when honored guests arrive, the villagers will gather in front of the drum house to conduct ceremonies. Usually, a drum house is of wood—its parts joined by lock brackets; no iron nails are needed. It may have four, six or eight columns square at the bottom; some, hexagonal. The drum house may have multiple eaves of three, five, seven or even fifteen, like a pagoda. The grand-looking drum house is the hallmark of a village.

The Wind-and-Rain Bridges are typical Dong

The Chengyang Bridge is the best preserved among all the Wind-and-Rain Bridges.

constructions found on almost every river. Among them, the most famous is the Chengyang Bridge in the Sanjiang Dong Autonomous County, Guangxi, which took over 20 years to complete: 76 meters long, 10.6 meters tall, 3.4 meters wide, with five piers and four arches each 14.2 meters long. This bridge, together with other three famous ones in China, is called the "four most famous ancient bridges in the country." Besides this bridge is another classic bridge, called Patuan in the Sanjiang. This was built in 1910, six years earlier than Chengyang, 50 meters in length, having one pier, two arches and three pavilions. Although not as large as Chengyang, this bridge has something very special. It has two levels, one for people and one for animals. This marvelous arrangement makes the bridge an ancient overpass. Each part of the bridge, pavilions and railings, is both attractive and highly functional, bearing proof of Dong people's wisdom and architectural skills.

About 2000-year old, the Yuanyang terraced fields in Honghe Prefecture, Yunnan, are the largest and the most spectacular of all terraced fields under the heaven.

Hani: Painting Masks for Heavenly Gods

◎ Thousand-Year-Old Terraced Fields
◎ Mushroom Houses

The Hani people live in the lower Lancang (Mekong) River reaches in south Yunnan, with a population of 1.43 million. Their places are high, between 800 and 2,500 meters above sea level. Most of the Hani people farm on terraced fields, which might have 100 terraces. These fields gave birth to a unique "terraced-field culture."

Lands in Yunnan and Guizhou Plateau are hilly. The ingenious Hani people made ditches on the slopes of a hill like silver ribbons to preserve rainwater. Even in a place 2,000 meters above sea level, growing rice is possible. The Hani people are very economical about soil, leaving not a bit unattended, even the smallest crack between two rocks. Their largest fields are about an acre, the smallest just a square foot. Fields in different sizes, like high and low notes, contribute to an airy melody.

Before each field is made, rocks are cut from different areas and shipped by hand to form a dyke on a selected slope. Because of the steep slope, some dykes may be as high as a meter.

The Hani people's terraced fields present a spectacular view, covering several counties. Just in Yuanyang, there are as many as 30,000 acres. Some slopes may have over

Hani terraced fields are an artwork, a man-made wonder under the heaven.

The Hani people have made a perfect unity of mounts, water, fields, forests and man.

3,000 terraces, from 700 meters up to 1,800, crisscrossing like a cobweb, the bigger one about half an acre and smallest, table-sized. With the variation of seasons, these terraced fields present magnificent views: tender green in spring, golden in autumn when all the rice is ready for harvest, like numerous mirrors in winter against the sunshine or silk ribbons hanging from the sky.

These terraced fields, together with forests, villages and water supply, make a local ecological system. Their distribution of water is both unique and scientific, quantity supplied depending on the labor input from each household in the building and maintenance of a ditch. Each household has a wooden plate, marked with the quantity of water the household is allotted, which is placed at the opening from the main ditch.

Their terraced-field culture is seen in every part of local people's life. People's names are inspired from the fields and a ceremony is held in the fields when a baby is born. If it is a boy, a seven- or eight-year-old boy is invited over, with a small hoe, to mimic the opening up of land. If it is a girl, a seven- or eight-year-old girl is invited over to mimic catching eels or

In their best, the Hani people are singing and dancing to celebrate their national festival.

shells in a paddy field. Only after this ceremony does the
newly born receive a name and become a village member.
The Hani people work in the fields throughout their lives
and, after death, are buried on the slopes by the terraced
field, to observe these lands forever.

Mushroom houses of the
Hani people.

Another unique thing about the Hani people is their
"mushroom houses." They are built around the terraced
fields. People say their ancestors, after seeing mushrooms
growing in wilderness, were inspired and created these
houses, which have earthen walls and bamboo shelves
cushioned with grass. Their roofs have four facets,
looking just like a mushroom. A mushroom house may
have three floors. The first floor is to store animals and
farming tools. The second floor is sectioned into three
rooms with a fireplace in the middle. The third floor has
an earthen roof, which is fireproof and good for more
storage. In winter, it is warm and in summer, cool.

Street-long festival
banquet of Hani people.

Miao: Wearing History On Costumes

◎ Chiming Silver Ornaments
◎ Graceful Wax Printing
◎ Elegant Pictures on Woven Brocade

One of the most ancient ethnic minorities in South China, the Miao people have undergone several major migrations in history. Today, among the 8.94 million people, most live in Guizhou, Hunan, Yunnan and Guangxi. The Miaoling and Wuling Mountains, where many of them live, have a mild climate, green hills and rapid rivers and yield many crops, such as rice, corn, millet, wheat, cotton, tobacco, canola and tung trees. In addition, these areas have much mineral and forest resources.

What makes the Miao people known is their handicraft works: silver ornaments, wax printing and woven brocade. Among them the silver ornaments, of many varieties, best demonstrate the Miao people's personality. In addition to the silver headwear, they have silver pins, bracelets, combs and small but equally exquisite plates to wear on their chests. Their largest silver horn may be 85 cm wide and 80 cm tall, over half of the height of its wearer. The Miao girls will decorate these silver horns with beautiful white feathers. Their silver headwear has many kinds of patterns, all elaborately wrought. When wearing such an ornament, the woman appears elegantly regal.

Wearing silver objects all
over their bodies.

The making of silver ornaments is done by hand, following an elaborate design by an artist. It takes over 30 steps from designing, carving, welding, inlaying and polishing before a piece is finished.

The silver decorative objects fall in many kinds, all elaborately wrought and indispensable to women's holiday wear.

Their wax printing is also famous. First, a piece of white cloth is placed on a table and wax is put inside a small pot to be heated until it melts. The melted wax is applied to the cloth, following no design but only imagination and birds, flowers, insects or fish are painted. After the painting is complete, the cloth is dyed and rinsed clean. Plants are the source of their dye: blue, yellow, red and black. The blue and white are major tones. A finished piece may have patterns as fresh as the azure sky, as white as the clouds, and as lively as the water running down a mountain, exhibiting a simple, elegant and national style.

The Miao people have woven brocade of their own features, called Miao brocade. Most of their patterns have

All silver decorative objects are hand-made,
taking much skill and high in artistic value.

Intelligent Miao women are working on wax-printing patterns.

Wax-print being dried up.

geometrical shapes, animals, plants, nature or images from ancient tales. The Miao women use bright color threads for a strong contrast. A finished piece, though just about 30 cm wide, is highly decorative, and is often chosen as skirt material.

Silver ornaments, wax printing and Miao brocade make their clothing special. As their clothes possess

a strong sense of history and express their feelings, their clothes are called "history books worn on body" or "clothing totems."

Miao women's apron.

Miao embroidery features great patterns and awesome colors.

Naxi: The Last Land of Women

◎ Strange but Romantic Weddings
◎ Grand Ceremony for Adulthood
◎ *Dongba* Culture—The Naxi People's Encyclopedia

As a branch of ancient Qiang, the Naxi people migrated many times until they eventually settled down in present-day Naxi Autonomous County in Yunnan Province. Some can be found in other counties, some even in Sichuan. Their population is about 300,000.

Ancient town of Lijiang, hometown of Naxi people.

Naxi women are known for being hard-working, virtuous and kind-hearted, their clothes are characteristic, meaning "wearing the moon and stars on their bodies."

In matrimonial and family life, the Naxi people still preserve the customs from the matriarchal society. For this reason, their homeland is called "the last land of women" on earth. The Naxi people in Yongning County of Yunnan, claiming to be "*Mosuo*," are most typical. In a *Mosuo* family, a female, the woman of the eldest generation, dominates. She is in charge of everything in the family: production, life, food and clothing. She also leads a family worshipping ceremony. Generations are counted only on the maternal side by the blood lineage of female generations, so the family's heritage is only available for female members. Following these principles, they have a marriage form called "*azhu*."

Azhu means "friend" or "mate." An *azhu* relationship does not involve a wedding ceremony. Any young man outside the bloodline can select a date from that family. So long as both are happy, and after exchanging simple

tokens such as bracelets or belts, they can live together at night but separate during the day. This is called *azhu* relationship. Such a relationship is very flexible, separate of concerns of family background, age and social status. It is a relationship not bound by law. When young people reach the age of 18, they can have an *azhu* partner. After meeting at work or on other occasions, they arrange a time and a secret signal for dating. The boy leaves his shoes at the girl's doorway to indicate that the girl is taken. If the two get along well, after a period of time, the two make their relationship known to others. As they live in different families, the young man only meets the

Muoso woman on the Lugu Lake.

Ceremony for adulthood of Mosuo girls.

girl at night and hurriedly leaves before dawn. Such a relationship may last for several years, or even longer. Some short relations may last just a year or several months. Most people have *azhu* experiences when they are young. As they grow older, they may have a stable relationship with just one. A girl may have more than one *azhu*, taking one as long-term while others are temporary. So does a young man. Children born from such a relationship has the girl's family name and is taken care of by the girl's family. Her brothers, in the father's capacity, shoulder the responsibility of education. In an *azhu* relationship, the male has no duties for raising or educating the children so such a relationship does not have economic ties. Their "divorce" is quite simple. So long as the girl refuses the boy's entry, it is finished. All she has to do is to move his belongings out. At this gesture, the young man leaves without ill feelings. Disputes or grudges seldom occur.

Meanwhile, the Naxi people attach great importance to the ceremony for adulthood, which involves an interesting ritual.

This ceremony is held when a child is 13 years old and is called "skirt-wearing ceremony" for a girl or "pants-wearing ceremony" for a boy. Before the children reach this age, they wear only hemp robes. The ceremony is held inside the mother's room. Inside each family's house, the mother's room is the main room in which two poles are placed—the left one is for a boy and the right one, a girl. The two poles are cut from the same tree. The ceremony for a girl is very grand, attended by all the family members. After blessing words are said, the mother helps the girl to change out of her old hemp robe into a new, beautiful and pleated flower-patterned skirt. Then, a sorcerer prays to ancestors on the girl's behalf before he hangs a wool necklace around her neck. After the ceremony, the rope is placed on a wooden pole

Dongba sorcerer doing drum-dance in Lijiang, Yunnan.

above the family shrine. In doing so, Naxi people say, the child will be tied to the family and live a long life. As the rope is wool, it is meant for her to remember forever the ancestors who reared livestock.

The ceremony for a boy is equally exciting. However, different from the one for a girl, the boy holds a knife and coinage in his hand, meaning from that day, he will have sufficient food and clothing. The ceremony is usually led by his uncle on his mother's side. After he changes into pants that symbolize adulthood, elder generations and relatives give him presents. The boy pays his respects to the ancestors' shrine, listens to sutra reading by a sorcerer and sings a song with other people.

Mysterious and ancient Dongba scripts.

All ceremonies have a sorcerer present. The Naxi people believe in a thousand- year-old local religion, called *Dongba*. This religion records almost every major events in history like an encyclopedia, covering local geography, history, medical practice, rearing livestock, food, habits and local customs. The *Dongba* language is pictographic, each character resembling a meaningful

picture. Even though someone may be able to read these characters, he may not understand the sutras. For this reason, the *Dongba* sorcerers who are able to read sutras and are knowledgeable in other fields, are important messengers of the Naxi culture.

The ancient Naxi music, a living fossil.

Qiang: Watchtowers in Hengduan Mountains

◎ **Watchtowers**
◎ **Ancient Paths**
◎ **Rope Bridges**

The Qiang people have a long history, very active 3,000 years ago in China's northwest and central plain. Today, most live in Sichuan, with a population of 300,000.

Most Qiang people farm, grow fruit and rear livestock. Several generations of a family often live together. The Qiang people believe in a primeval religion, taking

Qiang village, comprising watchtowers and residential houses, a typical Qiang construction complex.

white rocks as their god, which can be seen on lintels, on windows, in watchtowers and in forests. Legend has it that in ancient antiquity, while migrating, the ancestors of Qiang people met a hostile alien tribe in the upper reaches of the Minjiang River. Alarmed by a god, the Qiang ancestors used wooden clubs and white rocks to frustrate the tribe's attack. Out of gratitude, but not knowing the identity of their savior god, the Qiang people took white rocks as their god ever since.

In high mountains and deep ravines where the Qiang people live, rocks are abundant, serving as building

Watchtower of Qiang people in Aba, Sichuan Province.

Ancient Qiang buildings.

material for watchtowers. These tall constructions are awe-inspiring, very strongly built with square or rectangular blocks. In history, these buildings functioned as a protective stronghold against foreign invasions or gang-fighting. The oldest watchtower is already 1,200 years old, the youngest having a history of 500 years. Most watchtowers have lost their tops, yet their defensive purpose is still seen. In general, watchtowers are either for a family or for a village. A family watchtower is not tall, just between 10 to 20 meters high, built against a mountain to connect the house in front or back. The village watchtowers are higher, about 50 to 60 meters tall

Sunning corn inside yard.

Rope bridge.

to protect the whole village members. Most of the Qiang villages are built on top of a mountain or half-way up, in a very perilous position with an open view.

The Qiang people use plank roads and rope bridges to connect to the outside world. Plank roads are built along the faces of cliffs by drilling holes to hold the planks. In ancient history, a plank road had very important military significance. Plank roads were built by either wooden planks in a place heavily wooded, or on rocky cliffs by drilling holes. The best preserved ancient plank road is on the north bank of Zagunao River in Wenchuan County, Sichuan Province. It is said to have been built by Jiang Wei, an army general from the State of Shu (221–263). It was enlarged during the Qing Dynasty (1616–1911) into a path 158 meters long, 0.4–2 meters wide, 10–20 meters above a very rapid river. It used to be the important path to western areas in upper reaches of the Minjiang River.

Crossing a river by suspended ropes was a courageous

act by Qiang ancestors. Suspended ropes are also called rope bridges, a skill mastered by Qiang ancestors 1,500 years ago. The Weizhou Rope Bridge in Wenchuan County over the Minjiang and Zagunao rivers was built during the Tang Dynasty, 100 meters long and 1.5 meters wide, is a thrilling experience to cross.

Slide-rope across the river.

Va: Drumbeats That Transcend History

◎ Thunderous Drumming
◎ Fascinating Dances

Va people's village, Yunnan.

The Va people are also called *Ava*, meaning people living on top of mountains. They are found in counties in southwest Yunnan, with a population of 390,000.

Most of them live between the Lancang (Mekong) and Nu (Salween) rivers, in south Nushan Mountains, a very mountainous area with few flat fields, called Ava Mountain. Having a complex climate, the place produces much wood, also being a habitat of many wild animals. The Va people maintain their history by carving wood, to which their life is closely related, as seen in their famous wooden drums.

These unique wooden drums, native only to the Va people, are viewed as the protection god with a supreme spiritual power. They are used for expelling evil spirits, for calling village members to attend a meeting, for delivering a signal for help in need, and, of course, for fighting a battle. A wooden drum is made out of a log 0.8 meters wide and 2 meters long.

In each of their villages, one or several places house the drums. These houses are also the symbolic buildings

A Va family.

Picking tea leaves.

of a village. A drum house is a sacred place, just like temples or monasteries for other ethnic groups. Inside a wooden drum house, there are usually two drums, a male and a female one made from different trees. The male drum is smaller than the female drum. The male drum gives a resonant sound while the female one sounds mellow and long.

It is an auspicious period beginning in December, when the "pulling drum" ceremony begins. This is a big festival for the Va people. "Pulling a drum" takes about 10 days. The village head and the village sorcerer, leading some people, go to the mountains at night. After choosing a fine tree, they offer sacrifices and fire gunshots to expel devils. After the sorcerer makes a few symbolic chops, young men begin to fell the tree. They work at night until the tree falls. The next morning, all the village members attired in their best clothes join them, and, following the directions from the village head, begin to pull the tree

Exciting hair-shaking dance.

towards their village. Men pull and sing, while the old and children deliver food, alcohol and water to them. When the tree arrives at the village, it is left outside for a couple of days, only after another ceremony is held, and, at an auspicious moment, the tree is pulled inside the village by all village members to the right place for carpenters to work on it. Usually, drum-making takes about 6 to 10 days.

After the "pulling drum," "jumping drum" follows as a celebration that goes on night and day, attended by everyone in the village. "Worshipping drums," another religious ceremony, falls in January. At the gunshot by the sorcerer, village members gather to begin a series of activities, in which people excitedly try the new instrument with huge sticks for four different kinds of sounds.

Va people's religious ceremony involving wooden-drum dance and ox-head sacrifice.

The Va people are born singers and dancers. Their place, Ava Mountains, is the home for songs and dances. In a festival, or on a big occasion like "pulling a drum" or building a house, the villagers will hold a big celebration to continue for several days. When a drum is ready, and satisfied with after trial, it will be moved into the drum house and raised onto a shelf. Everyone is eager to try it.

Whenever they hear drumbeats, the Va people will start dancing. Dancing movements, with an everlasting charm, come from their daily life and work as inherited from their ancestors.

Tujia: Living in High Mountains

◎ Joyful at Funerals
◎ Weeping at Weddings
◎ The Age-Old *Nuo* Opera

The Tujia people call themselves "*bi zi ka*," meaning "locally born and brought up." They live in west Hunan, Hubei, and some counties in Sichuan. Their population is 8.02 million.

Most of them farm, receiving much influence from Han people in economy and culture, but still preserve their own features, seen mostly in their special funeral,

High-raised houses of Tujia people, Hubei Province.

wedding ceremonies and art.

Their funerals are probably different from any other ethnic minorities'. "Be happy at a funeral and sad at a wedding" is an age-old tradition. Drumbeats, dancing and singing are common at a Tujia funeral. When an old man dies, he is believed to go to the heaven and his death is called "white happiness." Men and women, old and young, will beat drums all night in memory of the dead. Their funeral dance is called *"sa er he."* People in small groups, often several in each, will dance wildly inside a mourning hall to the rhythm of drumbeats and songs.

Usually, *"sa er he"* has a drummer and several dancers. By beating the drum's body, edge and side, the drum produces different sounds, at which the dancers change their moves and rhythm. The songs have varied contents: history, seasons, morality, love, children's rhymes or memories about the dead. Both the singers and dancers are highly focused, while spectators clap in an excited chorus.

Different from their happy funerals, the Tujia people have another unique custom: weeping at a daughter's wedding. While weeping, they sing about the sad feeling when leaving family members. The weeping begins a month before a wedding, and reaches its climax the night

Funeral dance is native only to Tujia people.

before. The bride's family chooses nine girls to sing with the bride. They sing different songs—some dedicated to parents, some dedicated to bothers and sister-in-laws, some denouncing the matchmaker who made all these happen. These weeping songs, commonly called "ten sisters' songs," are enough to move listeners to tears.

The *Nuo* Opera of Tujia people, the living fossil of Chinese operas, came from primeval religious ceremonies in ancient antiquity frequently seen in a Tujia village. Because of a strong sense of worshipping ancestors, the *Nuo* culture is well-preserved. "*Nuo*" means to expel evil spirits and devils. The *Nuo* Opera has been passed down not by books but by verbal teaching from masters to students. Besides a family teaching, learning from

Used to communicate with the super natural, such a place is often seen in Tujia households of Dejiang.

Xi lan ka pu, bright and colorful brocade takes superb skill to make.

Weaving *xi lan ka pu* is a must skill for every Tujia girl.

The oldest Tujia dance, named *mao gu si*.

experienced ones is a common practice. Among all the students, only the best gets the secret best skills. *Nuo* has separate units called *"tan."* Each *"tan"* has a troupe with teachers between six and twelve. Each troupe has a headman; the rest of the members are just like brothers. The headman must have a surprisingly good memory and remarkable performing skills. The *Nuo* troupes are active after the autumn harvest until the plowing season next year.

All actors in a *Nuo* Opera wear masks, which record

the Tujia people's history. In early years, characters in *Nuo* Opera could be distinguished by their masks. Most of the masks are wooden; some modern ones might be fabric. The patterns and colors on the masks vary greatly to bring out the character of the roles. A *Nuo* Opera is also a religious ceremony and is usually performed in three parts: opening altar, opening cave and closing altar. The opening and closing altar is to receive and see gods off, while the opening cave part is the story to be played. When someone is sick, struck by a misfortune, he may pray and make a vow to the *Nuo* gods. When he comes back to honor the vow, he brings sacrificial objects like joss sticks and paper offerings.

Zhuang: The Ethnic Minority of the Largest Population

◎ The Singing Festival
◎ Brocade Embroidery
◎ Raised Houses Sitting on Stakes

Having the largest population among all ethnic minority groups in China, about 16.17 million in total, most of the Zhuang people live in the Guangxi Zhuang Autonomous Region, some seen in Yunnan, Guangdong and Guizhou provinces.

Breath-taking scene along the Lijiang River.

Their vast homeland is also called "the sea of songs." All of them are good singers and on festivals, they sing to communicate and to express themselves. They hold a singing festival every year, called "*ge xu*," attended by hundreds of people. The festival has day singing and night singing, both following age-old rules. The day singing is held outdoor, by jade mounts and rivers, attended mostly by young people with a hope to find a date. The night singing, however, is held inside the village, meant to teach the younger generation the knowledge about farming, local life and history.

The singing festival falls twice a year, in spring and autumn, but the one on the third day of the third month by Chinese lunar calendar is much larger. By their custom, the third day of the third month is an occasion to mourn the dead, also an occasion for the old to tell the young their family history and rules. After the lecture, a picnic follows, then singing and amusement. This day singing has become a local holiday with well-organized festivities attended by the whole village.

Every year, before this festival, every one is busy

preparing, five-color glue-rice and colorful eggs made in each household and beautiful brocade balls made by young girls. On the festival, every one is in his/her best for a ceremony to memorize their singing goddess "Third Sister Liu," in the hope to get her blessing and a better singing skill. To them, the sister was an epitome of sincerity, beauty, love, wisdom and capability. After the ceremony, young people release their voice into duet singing, "talking" to the opposite sex to find a date.

Every Zhuang girl is a master singer and dancer.

Zhuang women's centuries-old weaving technique and tools.

To young people, the third day of the third month is a Valentine's Day. Young men and young girls meet, singing to express themselves and examining the other side's personality, capability and looks. While the two are doing so, their friends will gather around them to show support. At sunset, the two may find a quiet place to continue. If the girl is happy with the boy, she may toss him the silk ball she has made as a token of love.

Besides exciting Zhuang Opera performances, small

The silk ball is a token of love for young people of Zhuang nationality, to be tossed at a dating candidate on the singing festival.

High-raised residential houses.

but enjoyable commercial activities add much festivity to the occasion. However, the most fruitful in the wake of a singing festival is of course the happy marriage lock forged between those in love.

The Zhuang women are smart and handy. Because of them, the local Zhuang brocade enjoys an equal fame with the other three best kinds in China. Unique in making and over 1,000 years old, Zhuang brocade features very bright colors and superb skills, perfect for making clothes, quilt or hand bags.

The Zhuang people prefer raised wooden houses by mounts and rivers. Due to the local rainy weather, their houses sit on one-meter-high wood stakes, floored inside with boards. The space below the house is to keep domestic animals and also serves as storage. These raised wooden houses were a marvelous invention from their ancestors, perfectly good for local environments.

Li: At the Edge of the World

◎ Tattoos about to Disappear
◎ Dancing to Get Blessings

Most of the Li, an ethnic group south of the Nanling Mountains, 1.24 million people in total, are found in the middle and southern parts of Hainan Province.

Their history in the Hainan Island can be traced back to over 3,000 years ago. Today, on the bodies of some aged women, we still see remains of a very ancient practice, tattoos in face, on chest, hands or legs. Some people call these tattoos "Dunhuang frescoes on human bodies."

By custom, getting a tattoo marked the end of juvenile years and the beginning of adult life. Teenage girls received a tattoo on an auspicious day, done by an experienced old woman. Besides the girl's mother, there was a middle-aged woman present to provide assistance. The tools needed for tattooing were simple, just a vine needle, a small club and a bowl of dye.

There are different versions about the origin of this practice. A popular one ascribed the practice to their ancestors, believing that a woman without tattoos would be denied by ancestors after death, left as a homeless ghost in wildness.

Their tattoos vary from area to area and from clan to clan. Some women have complicated patterns in face, neck, body, arms and waist, while some preferred simple ones. Because the Li people have no written language, these tattoos contain their history and cultural information, also serve as the totem of their clan or

A Li woman in traditional costumes is sunning rice just harvested in.

the mark of identity. However, due to the impact of contemporary life style and the change of values, tattooing as an ancient practice is disappearing among the Li women. The existent few are priceless cultural relics.

Besides tattoos, the Li people's dances are very special, seen on wedding ceremonies, when building houses,

Primitive village of Li people in Hainan Island.

on festivals and during a slack season. Among their dances, the best known is called "getting fortune dance," a dance popular in Tongshi and Maoyang. March, July and October are auspicious "ox days" to Li people. The Li ancestors believed that everything fell to two kinds, good and bad. The ox day is good, and dancing in March brings fortune to their livestock. Dancing in July is good for rice to grow, bringing a bumper harvest of all crops that year. Dancing in October brings people fortune, good health and peace. Besides, the bamboo stick dance is also popular, featuring local customs. On a festival, or after crops are harvested in, people will dance this form to the rhythms from thick bamboos clapped by squatting people. Dancers advance, retreat and leap vigorously

Tattooing has a long history among Li people, but different branch has a different way of doing it. Nowadays, aged people still keep it.

Bamboo stick dance, very popular
among younger generation of the Li
nationality.

Age-old way to make Li brocade.

to the rhythm among the bamboos. This unique form, characteristic of the Li culture, has developed into a very enjoyable local performance often joined by excited tourists.

Gaoshan: Calls from Mount Ali

◎ Colorful Clothes
◎ Highly Spirited "Hair-Shaking" Dance
◎ Twin-Cups Wine Offered with Utmost Sincerity

The name of Gaoshan refers to all aboriginal people in China's Taiwan Province, including Amei, Taiya, Bunong, Lukai and Yamei in different areas who speak different dialects. Most live

Houses of Yamei, a branch of Gaoshan people.

Expressive costumes of Lukai, a branch of Gaoshan people.

Costume made with
hemp, cloth, shell and
beads, in the collection
of the Central University
for Nationalities.

in east Taiwan or in islands close to east China's coastline. Some Gaoshan people, about 4,000, live in Fujian Province.

The Gaoshan culture is best reflected in their clothing. In ancient times, as they took nudity as beauty, their ancestors wore nothing. The females wore a piece of cloth or a straw skirt to cover their private parts, while men wore animal fur around their waists. Nowadays, in addition to the tattoos on their faces and bodies, men like to wear beautiful feathers on their heads, and women like to wear flowers on their bodies decorated by shells. Those in Pingpu wear short hemp blouses and fur skirts. The material for their clothing, besides fur and tree bark, is homemade hemp with colored patterns. The clothing for those in other places share similarities. Taiya, Saixia and Amei peoples in north Taiwan have sleeveless shirts, wraps, blouses and waistbands. Bunong in central Taiwan wear deer-hide vests, chest pouches and black skirts. The Paiwan, Lukai and Beinan peoples in south Taiwan prefer long-sleeved shirts and mid-length skirts. Among all these groups, the Yamei people have the most primitive form of clothing. Their men wear front-buttoned short vests and T-shaped underwear, while women have vests and straight skirts. In winter, they have a piece of square cloth to wrap their bodies.

Shell blouses demonstrate Gaoshan people's artistic attainment; they are made of shells with small holes threaded together into vertical lines to decorate a blouse. Such a blouse takes as many as 50,000 to 60,000 shells,

All dressed up, they are singing and dancing.

requires much effort and is time-consuming. In the past, this blouse symbolized fortune and power and was worn only by a headman of a tribe or a clan. Presently, only the ethnic minority museum in the Central University for Nationalities and the anthropological museum of Xiamen University have one in their collections.

The Gaoshan women are good at dyeing hemp cloth. They like to decorate their blouse fronts, sleeves, scarves and aprons with exquisite embroidery or shells or objects shaped from animal bones. Their national clothing is mostly black, white, red and yellow, with decorative objects on different parts of clothing. Their national clothes are for holidays, and, usually, the Gaoshan people just wear Han-style clothes or Western-style suits.

The Gaoshan people have a long history of dancing. Their dances show different activities in life, such as fishing, hunting, wood cutting, weeding, harvesting, weddings and offering sacrifices. In general, their group dances fall in three categories: dances for a worshipping ceremony, dances for wine-drinking and dances of imitation.

Dances for worshipping ceremonies are performed by a group in an open space, numbering from double-digits to several hundred. Dances for wine-drinking are done on an improvised manner in a yard by only a small group. The dances of imitation are also for group dancers but are more spectacular. All the three categories use very few or almost no music instruments. Occasionally, they may use percussion to indicate the beginning or end of announcements, they shout for rhythm and they beat a gong as a signal to move forward or turn, while singing and dancing all the while.

The "hair-shaking" dance is popular among Yamei women in Lanyu Isle, a dance typically from an ocean culture. In the past, they never danced during the day. They only did it under the moonlight. In Lanyu, it is said that the humidity and brilliant sunshine leave the females with shapely, graceful bodies. All of them have jet-black, long hair and like to walk barefoot. On a moonlit night,

Grand Harvest
Ceremony.

they gather on a pebbled beach to do "hair-shaking" dance. In the beginning, they line up to sing while gently swaying, accompanied by the musical sounds of the pebbles when stepped on. Then, they hold arms, bend forward, flick their long hair forward, sing and step forward until the hair touches the ground. Then, slightly bending knees, they shake their heads vigorously back, sending their hair into the sky and letting it stand for a while before falling on their backs. In the hard life of that island, this dance gives them much comfort and joy. It is a way of displaying youth. The long, black hair flicked upward is like a blazing flame.

Except for the Yamei branch, all Gaoshan people like to drink. They drink to their heart's content on many occasions: wedding, birth, building a new house, festivals, farming, hunting, and fishing or for religious reasons. On their harvest ceremony, which falls in August when the moon is full, people bring wine and food from their homes to enjoy while watching singing and dancing. They use wooden, bamboo or pottery cups; among them, the wooden cups with engravings are the most special; they consist of two or three cups joined together at the base so that two or three can drink at the same time. The twin-cups can be seen frequently when guests are received or at wedding ceremonies. Two people stand shoulder to shoulder, one holding the cup with his left hand while the other one holding the cup with his right hand. They raise the cups together to drink. By drinking from such cups, the Gaoshan people show their friendship, sincerity and goodwill. Among Paiwan people, not only the newlyweds use these cups, friends and relatives use them too. Unless the two raise the cups at the same time, the wine inside will spill. This is a symbol of equality and partnership, a sign to share fortune and difficulties alike.

Distribution of the Ethnic Groups in China

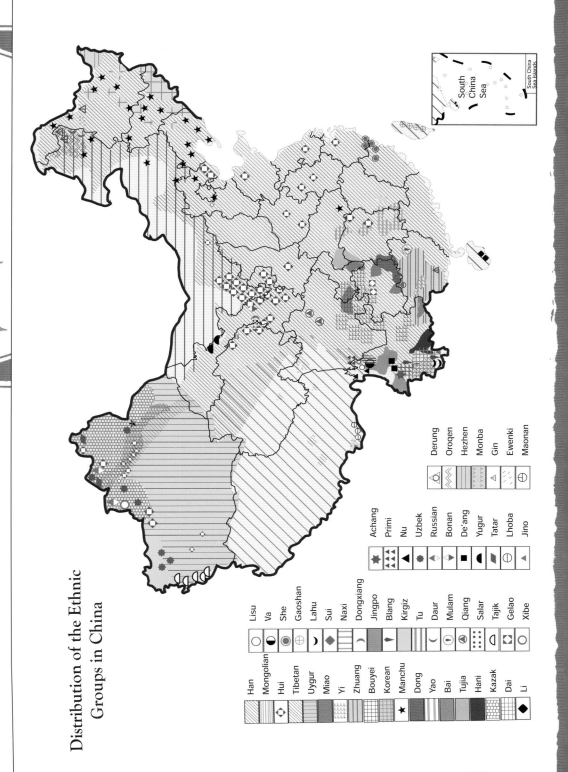

Han	Lisu	Achang
Mongolian	Va	Primi
Hui	She	Nu
Tibetan	Gaoshan	Uzbek
Uygur	Lahu	Russian
Miao	Sui	Bonan
Yi	Naxi	De'ang
Zhuang	Dongxiang	Yugur
Bouyei	Jingpo	Tatar
Korean	Blang	Lhoba
Manchu	Kirgiz	Jino
Dong	Tu	
Yao	Daur	Derung
Bai	Mulam	Oroqen
Tujia	Qiang	Hezhen
Hani	Salar	Monba
Kazak	Tajik	Gin
Dai	Gelao	Ewenki
Li	Xibe	Maonan

South China Sea

South China Sea Islands